My Big Book of
COLORING

Unicorn, Mermaid, and FairytaLe

OVER 40 Cool Illustrations

For Girl 4-8 Years Old

This CoLoring Book BeLongs to

Thank You For Getting Our Book!

If you find this ***Coloring Book*** fun and useful, we would be very grateful if you posted a short review on Amazon! Your support does make a difference and we read every review personally.

You would like to leave a review, just head on over to this book's Amazon page and click "Write a customer review".

Thank you for your support!

Copyright © 2020 by Frank Mallin